In this series –

RUMI READINGS
FOR
FAMILY

RUMI READINGS
FOR
FAMILY

JALALUDDIN RUMI

The Scheherazade Foundation

The Scheherazade Foundation CIC
85 Great Portland Street
London
W1W 7LT
United Kingdom
www.SF.Charity
info@SF.Charity

First published by The Scheherazade Foundation CIC, 2025

RUMI READINGS FOR FAMILY

© The Scheherazade Foundation

A CIP catalogue record for this title is available from the British Library.

ISBN 978-1-915311-71-9

Introduction

Jalaluddin Rumi was born in Balkh, Afghanistan, in the year 1207, and died in Konya, Turkey, in 1273.

During the sixty-six years spanning this pair of dates, he produced a range of extraordinary work in Persian which, today, is classed as 'Sufi Mysticism'.

In the seven and a half centuries since his death, Rumi's corpus, which includes *The Masnavi* and *Fihi Ma Fihi*, has been circulated widely across the Near East, the Arab world, and Central Asia.

Generations of students continue to commit selections of the 60,000 verses to heart, and allow Rumi's way of thought to permeate through all areas of their lives.

Although Orientalists venturing eastward from Europe in the 1700s occasionally made note of Sufi Mysticism, they tended to witness it through the more theatrical frills – such as 'whirling dervishes' – rather than through a deep appreciation of the texts.

It wasn't until the close of the nineteenth century that the first wholescale translations of Rumi's written work began to appear in Europe.

Even then, they remained very much the purview of a few academics, whose translations were – even for the time – laden with indescribably floral and cumbersome prose.

Although in the Occident, students would find themselves scrutinizing Rumi's corpus, it wasn't until more recently that accessible appreciations of his work became available.

A few years before his death, I asked my father – the Sufi scholar and thinker Idries Shah – for his thoughts on Rumi's legacy in the West.

Sitting in his favourite chair, a porcelain cup of green tea in hand, he looked at me hard.

'I never cease to be amazed,' he said.

'Amazed by what?'

'By the way people don't take what's perfectly packaged, and ready and waiting for them, but rather obsess with something else.'

'With what?'

'With endless and nonsensical trimmings, trappings, and paraphernalia.'

My father sipped his tea.

After a moment of silent thought, he continued:

'Read Rumi in the original Persian,' he said, 'and so delicate are the verses that you have tears rolling down your cheeks. Yet here in the West, it's served up as something submerged in a thick, glutinous gravy, so much so that its utterly inedible.'

I reminded my father that a series of publications had recently found their way to press – publications that presented Rumi's couplets in an utterly new way.

Stripped bare of what my father had referred to as 'gravy', they were light.

Indeed, they were lighter than light.

My father rolled his eyes at the thought.

'In any other place, and at any other time,' he said, 'people would be up in arms. Or, if they weren't, they'd be laughing until their sides split. Imagine it – Western poets with absolutely no knowledge of the original Persian text touting new, bestselling editions of Rumi's work! It's what we call "The Soup of the Soup of the Soup".'

In the years since my father's death, Occidental society has been flooded with all things Rumi.

Couplets ascribed to him are read solemnly at weddings across the United States, Europe, and beyond.

Wisdom drawn from his poetry is tattooed daily over the backs and limbs of Hollywood A-listers.

But the precious words uttered at weddings, tattooed into skin, and quoted in abundance, hold little or no bearing to the original verses of Jalaluddin Rumi.

So, there it is…

The great Sufi Master's wisdom available:

(a) in a form that's unreadable because it's all covered in glutinous gravy, or

(b) in another form that's completely distorted – the Soup of the Soup of the Soup.

One thing that *is* evident is that the West can benefit enormously from a clean, clear rendition of Rumi's thinking – as the East has done over the last seven hundred years.

For this reason, we have commissioned entirely new translations, gleaned in particular from *The Masnavi*. Selected and translated by native Persian-speaking scholars, the emphasis has been on maintaining the lightness of Rumi's poetry.

In an age of relentless speed and digital overload, and so as to allow the work to be accessed by those who may benefit from it most, we have arranged a series of bite-sized morsels by way of theme.

We encourage you to do what students, scholars, and ordinary people have done across the East for centuries...

To pick a single couplet, or a handful – and to read them over and over, allowing them to seed themselves in your mind.

Little by little, having taken root, they will blossom and bear fruit.

Tahir Shah

How to Use This Book

Rumi Readings for Family

Family is where we first learn to speak – and also where we often learn silence.

It is where love is formed, and where love is tested.

Where belonging begins – and where, sometimes, the deepest wounds are hidden.

This book is for anyone trying to understand what it means to belong to others, and to oneself, within the structure – and sometimes the chaos – of family life.

It is for parents and children, siblings and spouses.

For those who feel held by family, and those who feel hurt.

For those building families of their own, and for those trying to repair what's broken in the one they were given.

Rumi Readings for Family offers a way to see these relationships from a deeper vantage point – through the timeless wisdom of Jalaluddin Rumi, freshly translated from the original Persian by scholars working with The Scheherazade Foundation.

These quotes are drawn especially from *The Masnavi*, a masterwork of spiritual psychology, and arranged into ten thematic parts. They explore the foundations of family, the roles of parents and children, the dynamics of nurture and discipline, love and loss, togetherness and separation.

They do not offer solutions.
They offer insight.
They do not give rules.
They give reflections.

Let them work quietly – the way love sometimes does.

A Mirror for Every Role

This book is not just for one kind of reader. It speaks to many.

If you are a parent, it may help you hold your child more gently – or more wisely.

If you are a child, it may help you see your parents with more complexity – or more compassion.

If you are a sibling, it may give you words for a bond that often goes unspoken.

If you are estranged, grieving, exhausted, healing – these quotes may help you name what has never been fully named.

Family is not static. These words can meet you wherever you are in the journey.

One Quote at a Time

You do not need to read this book in one sitting. In fact, it may be best to let it unfold slowly.

Read a single quote at a time – in the morning, before bed, during a quiet moment in the day. Sit with it. Read it again. Ask yourself:

- What does this remind me of?
- Who comes to mind as I read this?
- What's being stirred?

You may want to keep a journal nearby – to write down your thoughts, your memories, your questions.

Read It Together - Or in Silence

Some readers may choose to use this book alone. That's a powerful path.

Others may choose to share it with a family member - a parent, a partner, a child - reading a quote aloud and talking about what it brings up.

Others may use it as a shared anchor across distances - a quote texted between siblings, or read before a difficult conversation.

There is no single way to use this book. Let it find its way into your life as quietly or as openly as feels right.

Let the Silence Speak

Not every quote will feel clear. Not every insight will arrive quickly.

Some quotes may feel too sharp. Others may feel too vague. That's okay.

Let them sit. Let the silence between the words speak too.

Sometimes, Rumi reminds us, the most important part of a conversation is the listening.

Let that listening extend inward – to your own story, your own patterns, your own tenderness.

Family Is Not Always Easy

This book does not idealize family. It does not pretend everything can be healed by poetry.

What it offers is perspective – a spaciousness, a grace, a widening of how we see each other.

It reminds us that family is not about control, or perfection, or performance.

It is about presence. About connection. About returning to love – even if love needs to be reshaped.

Rumi writes in this volume:

'Contemplate the possibility of having four eyes instead of the usual two, and provide assistance to your partner by using your own eyes. A partner offers assistance and protection along the journey; look more closely, for the partner is the same as the path itself.'

Let this book be the extra set of eyes.

Let it walk beside you as you try – gently – to understand, to forgive, to begin again.

Part 1
The Foundation of the Family

1

Lament the cruel companion!
Lament!
Find yourselves a reputable partner,
O beloved people.

2

Gender can be understood
as a certain perspective
that leads to various ways
in which individuals interact with one another.

3

Logic informed him
that authentic gender resides in meaning,
not in water and matter.
Do not idolize superficial appearances,
and refrain from such statements.
Explore the essence of gender
beyond physical appearance:
the form is like an inert rock,
devoid of life;
the lifeless entity is oblivious
to the concept of gender.

4

If we are inclined towards
something unnecessary,
it may resemble the necessary,
but only in a counterfeit way.
That which bears a resemblance
to the fundamental is taken from somewhere.
And that which is taken from elsewhere,
will not last forever.

5

To prevent falsehood from dissipating;
to safeguard against deception by a distorted idea.

6

Certainty is the state of being confident and assured,
particularly in the enjoyment and satisfaction
derived from one's own kind.
It involves perceiving the interconnectedness
and interdependence of each component
in relation to the entirety.

7

Wisdom is able to distinguish
between similarities and differences,
and is not easily influenced
by superficial appearance.

8

Virtue is naturally attracted to goodness;
wickedness is inherently associated with evil.
Be aware!
For bitterness will always align with bitterness.
When will deception ever be united with Truth?

9

The heart guides you towards others
who possess compassion and empathy,
while the physical body limits you to matters
pertaining to the material world.

10

From the world of perception and insight
forms of the same kind are clearly seen.
The manifestations of 'male' and 'female'
emerge from the domain of perception.
Associate with individuals who possess enlightenment,
as there exists a means of communication
between their hearts.
Both challenge and joy on Earth
can be found in water.

Part 2
Forming a Family

11

At home there is a perpetual search
for the essential requirements to survive:
water, bread, social standing.
In such manner, the soul tries to find resolution,
sometimes mundane,
sometimes seeking domination.

12

Her captivating beauty ensnared men,
causing them to lose both reason and patience.
On seeing those eyes brimming with intoxication,
their intelligence and wisdom became unsettled.

13

Avoid dedicating yourself to material riches
and pursuing romantic relationships,
as these pursuits divert one's attention away
from spiritual matters.

14

Take care when confiding in individuals
who have close relationships with gossipers,
as these two factors bring volatility.

15

Cease your subservience,
O spirit,
for this charade masks the absence of genuine meaning
with deception and cunning.

16

A partner infatuated
with physical attractiveness and charm
determines their own course through life.
In the perspective of such a one,
the concept of Truth becomes a mere illusion
among fellow human beings.

17

Although you command concealment,
a wish for self-display grows stronger,
and the desire of others becomes greater.

18

Cursed is the one
whose thoughts are focused solely on material matters,
whose repulsive soul is forceful and on guard.
Their mind is inevitably overpowered,
and their words yield only detriment.

19

See the mind as illumination,
your desire as greed and longing.
These two only obscure and bewilder,
while mind serves
as the source of enlightenment.

20

They manipulate the heart to desire
and obscure its vision,
causing the donkey to seem as radiant as Joseph's fire.
They see themselves as the ultimate source of light,
despite being consumed by fire and misery.

Part 3
Responsibilities in the Family

21

They triumph over ignorant partners
whose disposition is like that of an animal.

22

As the proverb says on the relationship
between a husband and wife:
A man must not maltreat his partner.

23

Handle them with kindness
to ensure the preservation of your greatest possession,
shielding them from ruin and arrogance.

24

Like someone with two partners,
one of whom causes immense pain,
while the other holds a more cherished place in the heart:
treat them as if they were more delightful
than anything else.

25

Without my patience,
you would have to endure the burden of a tiresome partner.
When did you take away my defenseless lion?

26

They thought about their actions towards others,
and faced the consequences imposed by life.
I wanted to incite jealousy in others,
but instead, they approached me,
and fell into a well.

27

Whenever anyone without authorization
passes through my entrance,
the inhabitants of the sanctuary
are concealed behind the curtain.
But when a trustworthy person enters,
they are allowed through these barriers.

28

If you encounter a person
who has observed or has a romantic relationship
with you within your home,
and they conceal themselves from your presence,
refrain from revealing my existence to anybody,
as it embarrasses me.
It is always inappropriate to display them publicly
and extend invitations for others
to witness this magnificence.
The lover would be pleased,
but you would experience anger.

29

Seek food using the appropriate channels
in order to pass through the doors of your country
and enter its gates.

30

He faced the city and asked:
'Master, do you not visit the village to have fun?'
Call out the children,
for this is like a flourishing garden
and the season of spring.
Or else you might come during the summer,
at harvest season,
for me to provide you with attentive service.

Part 4

Woman as Mother

31

The extraordinary power of a mother
lies in her ability to give voice to a voiceless child
through nothing more than her breath.

32

She is a source of abundant vitality;
take water from her for the growth of new plants.
We engage in the discourse of holy individuals,
consuming the wisdom and teachings of Khidr.[1]
Approach, O ignorant one in need of watering!

---

1   'The Green One': a spiritual guide in Islamic tradition.

33

The mother takes the role of the one
who actively searches for her offspring
while the roots provide support to the branches.

34

As a mother quivers with fear for her child,
we quiver with fear for our faith.
Why does she shake,
this fragile being that embodies pure belief?

35

When a mother tells you,
'I hope you die!'
she is only expressing a desire
for the elimination of negative behaviour,
or moral decay.

36

On becoming a mother,
her child becomes the focal point of her attention,
and receives all her affection.

37

I direct my gaze not towards you,
but rather towards the depths of your heart;
I present a gift to her,
the essence of my being.
I am in the same position as you
when it comes to being with her;
the skies are beneath the feet of our mothers.

38

The woman's elegance shifts
in the direction of the origin;
she discovers solace
in the presence of her mother.

39

It was said that those who were not deserving
did not contribute to your success,
but they caused it to become excessive and prolonged.
Each undeserving individual caused you to fall ill.
Seek solace in the embrace of your mother,
for she will provide you with care and healing.

40

The infant quivers in response to the sting,
like a leech.
The empathetic mother finds delight
in that sadness.

Part 5

The Roles of Parents in Nurturing Children

41

Engage with children!
It is through you that they develop their ability to speak.

42

With each newborn
a parent should take care,
as though handling a delicate and
complex puzzle.

43

The mother calls to her child,
'Come here!'
The child replies,
'But why must I drink my milk?'

44

The child naturally strives for stability
and active functionality;
without them,
it lacks secure foundations.

45

For children the word 'game'
can only mean one thing:
play and fun.

46

When returning from the edge of the ocean,
be mindful of your need for water.
By engaging with toys,
a child's understanding of fundamentals
develops, step by step, in playfulness.

47

As a sail appears weightless above a ship,
so love becomes eternal when reciprocated.
Step closer to the young child
who instinctively pulls away to avoid falling over.

48

Giving bread instead of milk to a child
may deprive them of essential sustenance,
and puts their health at risk.
Once they develop teeth,
they will naturally desire solid food,
like bread, for nourishment.

49

Legal contracts are not applicable to those
who are drunk or mentally unstable.
In a like manner, children are exempt
from legal responsibility.

50

The legitimacy of a child's laughter and tears
holds little meaning without context
or understanding.

Part 6
How to Be a Child

51

A mother's compassion,
bestowed by God,
commands devotion and duty.

52

If their heart is content with you,
then I am content.
If they express dissatisfaction towards you,
then I also express dissatisfaction.

53

The mother's right stems from her noble responsibility
for you since your very conception.
He created a physical structure within her body,
granted her tranquility
and endurance during her pregnancy.
The Creator has bestowed on to the mother
a multitude of talents and abilities
with the intention of eliciting an outpouring
of love for you.

54

Observe Moses,
the offspring of Imran,
who departed to Midian out of concern for his mother
and attained mastery through that journey.

55

While the mother is characterized by her compassion,
one can observe the divine kindness in the father's anger.

56

Thanks to my harmonious relationship with my father,
I perceive this world as Paradise.

57

If you are loyal to someone
other than your mother and father,
where does your relationship with them stand?

58

The prayer that is mandatory and certain,
serving as the beginning and end of all utterances,
is the prayer dedicated to the mother and father
who foster and cultivate this young plant.
May God protect them within the refuge of His grace,
just as they nurtured this feeble individual
under the guardianship of their concern.

59

Nevertheless, as your parents have designated you
as a mediator
by agreeing to raise and care for you,
(and as a result of this agreement,
the numerous blessings have been evident
in your physical being),
it is now incumbent upon you
to express gratitude to them:
'Be grateful to Me and to your parents.'

60

The daughter expressed her willingness
to assist her father:
'I find your counsel gratifying,
and advantageous to my emotional well-being.'

Part 7

How Parents Should Behave with Their Children

61

The pea was willing to be boiled
only if the pot could cook it in the right way.
Similarly, you are like my creator:
move me, then, as you skilfully perform your task.

62

Every year a mother gave birth to a son,
but none survived beyond six months.
Several died
before the age of three or four months.
and she cried,
'Oh Lord, come to my aid!'
That night, she was shown a paradise
that was green and everlasting, cheerful, and effortless.

63

The young horse said,
'These people are making fun of me.
Their ridicule overwhelms me with sadness.
My heart is vexed and trembles;
their roaring insults fill me with anxiety.'
The mother answered that those who offend have existed
since the beginning of the world.
So perform your duties diligently, O beloved,
for in due time they will be ensnared by their own traps.

64

He seized the infant and threw him into the flames.
The woman was frightened, and her faith wavered.
She wished to prostrate herself in front of a deity,
but the young child exclaimed,
'I am still alive!
Mother, please come in.
I am content in this place,
despite being surrounded by flames.'
The fire serves as a concealment for the eye,
but mercy is the benevolent outcome
that has arisen from its covering.

65

The mother's spirit warns the bright-eyed youngster
that only grief and regret would result from this situation.
Free yourself from the clutches of this nurturer
and her affectionate gestures;
a mother's physical reprimand
is preferable to her indulgent treats.

66

But take care to prevent your children
from being devoured by an elephant.
Offspring are fragile, delicate
and vulnerable,
and a mother is always watchful and prepared
to protect them.

67

His mother admonished him furiously,
'Silence!
Who whispered this to you?
By whom were you instructed in this, young child?
How did you acquire such a refined,
and articulate command of language at such a tender age?'
The child replied,
'I was instructed by God, and then by Gabriel.
When it comes to speaking,
I act as a messenger alongside Gabriel.
The one who possesses knowledge of God
is genuinely recognized,
and his name remains steadfast in Truth.'

68

The fingernail, crucial for work, for hunting,
is haphazardly trimmed by the blind old woman.
Where was the mother
when your nails reached such a length?
She trimmed the eagle's nails, beak, and feathers;
this is the action of an elderly woman
driven by affection.

69

One killed his mother in a fit of rage,
using both a knife and his bare hands.
Another, with malicious intent,
accused her of neglecting her mother's duties.
'What drove you to matricide?'
they asked.
'What actions did she undertake to warrant such an end?'
'I took her life in order to protect her
from the violence of others.
Her flute is superior to that of the people.'

70

Summon, O affection,
in the interest of the lives of your offspring,
annihilate thoughts with that wine,
like sparks issuing from a fire.
Yesterday, you bestowed your gift,
gathering everything,
O magnanimous benefactor.
Please grant today's gift
as you are perpetually giving.

Part 8

Features of
Happy Families

71

Words used in intimate situations
differ from those of regular communication,
as empathy surpasses simple verbal exchange.

72

Contemplate the possibility of having four eyes
instead of the usual two,
and provide assistance to your partner
by using your own eyes.
A partner offers assistance and protection
along the journey;
look more closely,
for the partner is the same as the path itself.

73

If you wish to shine like daylight,
burn your Self into the darkness of night.
You have firmly grasped the concepts of 'me' and 'mine';
yet only devastation comes from duality.

74

The agony experienced by a friend is limitless,
as it lies at the very center,
while friendship serves as the outer husk.
Genuine friendship entails more than feelings of happiness;
it involves facing difficulties and pain together.
A friend is like gold
that has been subjected to intense heat,
as it is only through this process
that the true value and purity of the metal is revealed.

75

Through the goodness of a friend
our difficulties are transformed into a source of solace
sweeter than sugarcane.
If a grain of that sugar were to fall into water,
the harsh taste of the sea
would be forever changed.

76

Escape the constraints and free yourself,
child.
How much longer will you remain enslaved
by material wealth?
If you were to pour all the water in the sea into a jug,
what would its full capacity be?
Merely part of a single day.

77

Actions that originate from your heart and soul
should be embraced and cherished,
just as you would cradle your own child.

78

Their affairs are determined
through collaboration and discussion,
ensuring that mistakes and deviations are avoided.

79

Renounce your personal inclinations
and instead prioritize the preferences of others,
as the appreciation of someone who expresses
thanks endures.

80

When arguing to foster growth,
every complaint reveals its appreciation.
Conflicts arise to correct the course;
the snake-catcher actively seeks companionship
with the serpent.

Part 9

Factors Influencing the Separation of Couples

81

Your love encompassed all that existed,
embellished with the essence of Truth, like gold.
When the gold lost its inherent qualities,
and mere brass remained,
interaction moved towards separation.

82

If the son of a king betrays his father,
his head is cut from his body.

83

Discord emerges as a result of disagreement;
victory emerges as a result of unity.
When both you and your spouse display scornful behaviour,
the intensification of contempt
leads to the breakdown of the relationship.

84

A friend desires happiness and pleasure,
as the wish stems from your preferences.
A friend should not be seen
as an object that can be easily damaged.
When you betray or hurt them,
it causes a rupture in the relationship.
The audible cracking sound produced by wood
is a result of its separation.

85

An enemy using sorcery causes
a deterioration in appearance,
resulting in the dissolution of the marital union.

86

The woman confronted her husband,
demanding to know why his attentiveness
had so suddenly vanished.
'Why do you show no concern for me?' she asked.
'Why must I endure this disgrace alone?'
He replied, 'I provide for our needs,
despite the challenges I face.
My dear, I supply nourishment and clothing,
But these alone do not truly care for you.'

87

The husband said,

'Dear wife, allow me to ask you a question:

As a destitute man, poverty is my sole expertise.

This is a harsh, nasty, and unpleasant situation,

yet it is important for you to ponder carefully,

my beloved.

Which is more severe, the adversity and unpleasantness,

or the act of divorce?

Which of these options do you find more unpleasant:

this situation, or separation?'

88

Bestow upon the unfaithful
a multitude of divorces,
as their mere presence
will deplete your vitality.

89

Disregard the insignificant acts of rudeness,
and choose to forgive without seeking revenge.
Pledge that you would not entertain thoughts of division,
but instead exert effort towards unity and reuniting.

90

Make every effort to prevent divorce,
as divorce is what I despise most.

Part 10

The Quality of Sibling Relationships

91

A subtle yet profound connection is unveiled
between siblings,
serving as a window from heart to heart.
Those unaware of this inner perspective,
regardless of their intelligence,
are deemed inexperienced and ignorant.

92

In siblings, both water and fire coexist,
though their origin is merely stone.

93

Brothers and sisters
share a deep affection,
as they all possess a unified essence derived
from their close bond.

94

Come forth from the extraordinary days,
where concepts of brotherhood, parenthood,
and motherhood intertwine
in pursuit of peace.
May I inquire about your esteemed identity,
as even the departed rise from their graves?
Brother, your noble reputation is not overpowering.

95

Even as Gabriel offers aid,
you stand guard like a brother.

96

He lost consciousness and bowed his head
upon arriving at the perfumers' market.
The tanner, who was his brother,
swiftly and cleverly made his way to the designated spot,
taking immediate action.
He kept his distance from others to shield them
from noticing his condition.
Discreetly, he shared confidential information with him,
then gently placed an object on his forehead.

97

It is better to keep your distance from a deceitful sibling,
and preferable to avoid a friend
with whom you are incompatible.
The mere presence of a compatible friend is superior
to the loyalty of a deceitful sibling.

98

If you lack concern
for hypocrisy and malevolence,
why harbour baseless suspicions towards your sibling?
Perpetual distrust detracts from attractiveness.
Examine your interactions as a true confidant.

99

On seeing his arrogance,
the Grand Mufti simply attributed some
responsibility to the person for the rebellion.
He criticized him for his excessive pursuit of profit,
even taking liberties, like cutting a portion of
a cypress tree without permission.
Where is your focus and reason,
O wine-drinker,
that you perceive knowledge as an adversary?
He noted that using offensive language
reflects one's character,
and that attitude can influence one's appearance.
Countenance should be like an unyielding iron surface,
candidly revealing even the sight of an unattractive face.

100

Just as one nurtures and loves a child or sibling
without hope of reward,
so, too, do they offer their generosity, loyalty, hope,
faithfulness, mercy, compassion and tenderness
without anticipating any personal gain in return,
unlike what may be expected in family relationships.

Finis